The Battle of the Little Bighorn

by Marc Tyler Nobleman

Content Adviser: Professor Sherry L. Field,
Department of Social Science Education, College of Education,
The University of Georgia

Reading Adviser: Dr. Linda D. Labbo,
Department of Reading Education, College of Education,
The University of Georgia

 COMPASS POINT BOOKS

Minneapolis, Minnesota

Compass Point Books
3722 West 50th Street, #115
Minneapolis, MN 55410

Visit Compass Point Books on the Internet at *www.compasspointbooks.com* or e-mail your request to *custserv@compasspointbooks.com*

Photographs ©: Hulton Getty/Archive Photos, cover, 9, 35; Stock Montage, 4, 5, 12; North Wind Picture Archives, 6, 10, 14, 15, 18, 25, 27 36 (top), 37 (right and left); Archive Photos, 8, 17, 30, 31, 32, 33, 36 (bottom), 39; Denver Public Library, Western History Collection, 19, 20, 22, 23, 24 (top and bottom), 28, 40, 41; Library of Congress, 26, XNR Productions, Inc., 34.

Editors: E. Russell Primm, Emily J. Dolbear, and Deborah Cannarella
Photo Researcher: Svetlana Zhurkina
Photo Selector: Linda S. Koutris
Designer: Bradfordesign, Inc.
Cartographer: XNR Productions, Inc.

Library of Congress Cataloging-in-Publication Data

Nobleman, Marc Tyler.
   The Battle of the Little Bighorn / by Marc Tyler Nobleman.
      p. cm. — (We the people)
   Includes bibliographical references and index.
   ISBN 0-7565-0150-4 (hardcover : lib. bdg.)
      1. Little Bighorn, Battle of the, Mont., 1876—Juvenile literature. 2. Dakota Indians—Wars, 1876—Juvenile literature. [1. Little Bighorn, Battle of the, Mont., 1876. 2. Dakota Indians—Wars, 1876. 3. Indians of North America—Great Plains—Wars.] I. Title.
   E83.876 .N63 2002
   973.8'2—dc21   2001001588

TABLE OF CONTENTS

America's 100th Birthday 4

Forced to Move 10

"Circus Rider" 14

Gold in the Hills 18

Another Civil War 23

Into Battle 27

Custer's Plan 31

Last Stand 35

Last Victory 38

Glossary 42

Did You Know? 43

Important Dates 44

Important People 45

Want to Know More? 46

Index 48

AMERICA'S 100TH BIRTHDAY

In 1876, as the United States turned 100 years old, exciting changes were in the air. In its first century, the country had grown to include thirty-seven states. Civil War hero Ulysses S. Grant had been elected the eighteenth president in 1868. Alexander Graham Bell had just patented his new invention—the telephone.

President Ulysses S. Grant

Nobody knew it yet, but automobiles and airplanes would be traveling across the nation in a few short decades.

Alexander Graham Bell opens the first phone lines from New York to Chicago.

The young country had its troubles, however. For
thousands of years, the North American continent had
been home to millions of Native Americans. Since the

5

Tensions with Native Americans increased as more settlers moved west.

Europeans first explored and settled North America, their relationship with the Indians had been tense—and often violent. The conflicts were usually about land. Hundreds of tribes of Native Americans had lived in the Americas before any white person ever set foot there. Imagine how the Indians felt when these newcomers tried to force them off their tribal grounds. Sadly, many settlers simply did not respect or understand the Native American way of life. This long conflict led to a series of wars that raged most strongly between 1866 and 1890.

The most infamous of these battles occurred on June 25, 1876—only nine days before the July 4 **centennial** celebration of the signing of the Declaration of Independence. That day the U.S. Army and a force of Native American warriors fought a bloody battle at the Little Bighorn River. The battleground was in Montana Territory, now the state of Montana.

The Battle of the Little Bighorn is also known as Custer's Last Stand. U.S. Lieutenant Colonel George Armstrong Custer made a big mistake that day. His mistake cost him his life as well as the lives of every man in his company. Custer's actions were neither smart nor heroic, but they made him an American legend.

The Battle of the Little Bighorn

Custer and his men fought their final battle at the Little Bighorn.

The Battle of the Little Bighorn was a great victory for the Indians—but it also marked the beginning of the end of the way of life they had enjoyed for centuries. Although the Indians won this famous battle, they would soon lose their homelands.

9

FORCED TO MOVE

George Custer was born in New Rumley, Ohio, on December 5, 1839. Nine years earlier, the U.S. government had passed the Indian Removal Act. That law required all

The Black Hills are sacred to the Sioux.

Native Americans to move off their homelands and make room for new settlements and for cotton fields. The Indians were forced to move west of the Mississippi River and live on reservations—land chosen and set aside for them by the U.S. government. A few years later, an area called Indian Territory was established in what is now Oklahoma. Tribes from the Southeast had to relocate there permanently. They were not given a choice—they were forced to move.

The Bureau of Indian Affairs (BIA) was formed by the U.S. government in 1824. Part of the agency's job was to move the Indians to reservations. This was not an easy task, however. First, the Indians did not want to leave their homelands, which were sacred to them, to live on government lands. Second, the reservations were sometimes hundreds of miles away. Many Native Americans got sick or even died while making the long trip. Third, the BIA constantly made agreements with the Indians— and then broke its own promises. For example, the U.S.

11

The U.S. Cavalry was often called in to control the American Indians.

government would suddenly take back land that had been promised to the Indians and use it to build railroads or start farms.

At that time, the government did not believe that forcing the Indians to move violated the Native Americans' rights. However, the Indians knew that nobody had the right to control their lives. They surely must have been thinking, "Why should we move? We were here first!" Many Indians were so angry and insulted that they refused to leave their land. In these cases, the U.S. **cavalry** was sent in to get them off the land, dead or alive.

All of these factors—the Indian Removal Act of 1830, the establishment of the Indian Territory in 1834, and the relocation orders—increased the tension between white settlers and Native Americans. These unjust actions set in motion the events that would lead to the tragedy at the Little Bighorn forty years later.

"CIRCUS RIDER"

In 1857, George Custer entered West Point, a distinguished military academy in New York State. He graduated in 1861, last in his class. The American Civil War, fought between the Northern states and the Southern states, had just begun. Custer was assigned to the G Company of the Second U.S. Cavalry.

The U.S. Military Academy at West Point, New York

Custer fought in the First Battle of Bull Run during the American Civil War.

Although Custer had not been a good student, he was a brave soldier. He fought in some of the most important battles of the war, including the First Battle of Bull Run in Virginia in 1861. He was a strong fighter on the

15

battlefield. He also seemed fearless, which earned him the respect of his commanding officers and his fellow soldiers. One soldier described him as "a circus rider gone mad!" Custer achieved the rank of brigadier general of volunteers at the age of twenty-three, making him the youngest American to receive that honor at the time.

Custer's appearance was somewhat out of the ordinary. His long, blond hair grew to his shoulders. He was also known for wearing a special uniform he had designed, which included lots of gold braid. Custer often had to be disciplined for his wild behavior—a trend that would continue throughout his military career.

After the Civil War ended in 1865, Custer served on the frontier with the Seventh Cavalry. The American frontier was a vast stretch of land west of the country's more settled areas. It was often called the Wild West. While with the Seventh Cavalry, Custer gained national attention as an Indian fighter. His service was interrupted in 1867 when he was **court-martialed**—tried by a military court—

Custer (left) with his wife and younger brother

for leaving his post in order to visit his wife, Elizabeth.

Custer returned to duty in 1868, however.

Gold in the Hills

By the mid-1800s, many white settlers were moving west in search of new opportunities. They regularly fought with the Native Americans they met along the way. Some of these Indians had already been forced to move west—now they had to fight, once again, for their lands. Other tribes,

Native Americans did not like white settlers moving into their homelands.

A Sioux family at a teepee camp in the Dakotas

such as the Sioux, had always lived in this part of the country. They were fighting to save their original homelands.

The Sioux were the largest and most powerful tribe on the Great Plains. They called themselves the Lakota or Dakota, words that mean "allies." The tribe included

An 1868 treaty gave the Sioux a huge hunting ground in the Black Hills.

many smaller groups, such as the Oglala of the Black Hills
of South Dakota, and the Hunkpapa of what is now
Montana.

Between 1866 and 1867, the U.S. Army and the Oglala Sioux had a series of **skirmishes** on the northern plains. These small wars stopped for a while in 1868. That year, the government signed a **treaty** that gave the Sioux their sacred hunting ground in the Black Hills of South Dakota. Sadly, six years later, the peace ended when something very valuable to the settlers was discovered in the region—gold. A struggle of a different kind was about to begin.

In 1874, George Custer violated the 1868 treaty. He entered the Black Hills with a group of 1,200 men in search of the precious metal. Custer and his men found what they were looking for—and, soon, many more men arrived in the region looking for gold of their own. Once the gold rush began, the government tried to buy the land back from the Sioux. The Sioux would not sell it, and so the government declared them to be "hostile."

The government then ordered the Sioux to relocate to distant reservations, even though winter was approaching.

Gold miners entered the Sioux territory in 1874.

Again, the government offered the Indians no financial help. Again, the Sioux refused to leave their lands, and again, violence erupted.

ANOTHER CIVIL WAR

Ten years after the American Civil War ended, the great Sioux war began. A civil war is a war fought between two groups in the same country. The great Sioux war was a civil war too. It was fought between Indians—the native Americans—and settlers—the new Americans.

Although leaders of the U.S. Army probably didn't know it, the Native American tribes had at last formed a

The U.S. Army invades a Sioux camp

23

powerful alliance. Two great chiefs joined together to lead their united tribes in the battles that were about to begin—Crazy Horse, chief of the Oglala Sioux, and Sitting Bull, chief of the Hunkpapa.

A large group of Sioux, many Cheyenne, and some Arapaho Indians gathered near the Little Bighorn River in

24

Sitting Bull, top. The Sun Dance, bottom.

Montana Territory. There they performed a sacred ritual called the Sun Dance. During the ceremony, Chief Sitting Bull had a vision. In his vision, he saw soldiers falling from the sky into the Sioux camp. He interpreted his vision as a sign that the Indians would defeat the U.S. Army.

Meanwhile, the army was preparing to drive out the Indians. Their plan was three-**pronged**, which meant that it called for three army **detachments,** or groups. Each group of soldiers would approach the Indian camp from a different direction in order to surround the enemy. The first group was led by General George Crook. The second was led by Colonel John Gibbon. The third was led by Brigadier General Alfred H. Terry.

General George Crook

William W. Belknap

Although he was known as a great Indian fighter, Custer was not involved in this campaign at first. He had recently **testified** in a court case against a man named William Belknap, who was President Grant's secretary of war. Belknap had been involved in the illegal sale of trading posts in Indian Territory. Grant was so angry that Custer testified against a member of his staff that he dismissed Custer from the army.

Custer was so popular with the public, though, that Grant had to reverse his decision. So Custer joined the campaign under Brigadier General Terry's command. The "circus rider" had cut his long hair and was ready for battle.

INTO BATTLE

The campaign began on June 17, 1876. General Crook led his men from the south. Colonel Gibbon's men marched from the west, and Brigadier General Terry's troops moved in from the east.

General Crook and his forces the day before the Battle of Rosebud

27

The Sioux lead a charge against part of General Crook's army.

Crook's group was the first to encounter Indians, at a place called Rosebud Creek. These Indians were led by Chief Crazy Horse. After the battle, Crook withdrew his soldiers to get more supplies. Meanwhile, Gibbon's and Terry's groups had met up with each other. Although they met near Rosebud Creek, neither commander knew about Crook's battle or his withdrawal. The three-pronged campaign had now become two-pronged.

Terry told Gibbon to approach the Indians from upstream. He instructed Custer and the Seventh Cavalry to cross the Little Bighorn River and advance from downstream. Knowing that Custer was reckless and often took chances, Terry gave him special written instructions. Custer was ordered not to make a move against the Indians until Gibbon was also ready to attack. Custer headed out for Little Bighorn River with about 600 soldiers.

Scout Bloody Knife (left) and Custer (second from left) with a grizzly bear in the Black Hills

CUSTER'S PLAN

On June 20, Custer located the Indian encampment. His Native American scout, Bloody Knife, warned him that it would be foolish—and probably fatal—to attack. The scout had seen about 3,000 Sioux, Cheyenne, and Arapaho warriors in the camp, ready for combat. These Indians formed

Major General Alfred H. Terry

the largest gathering of Native American warriors in recorded history. Custer and his Seventh Cavalry were

31

severely outnumbered.

On June 25, after an exhausting 40-mile (64-kilometer) march in the summer heat, Custer's troops got very close to the Indian camp. Custer prepared to attack immediately, ignoring Bloody Knife's warning and disobeying Terry's order to wait for Gibbon.

Captain Frederick Benteen

Custer had a plan, and he was sure that it would result in victory for the U.S. troops. At the time, Custer was a lieutenant colonel—just a few ranks lower than general. He was an experienced soldier and should have

32

known better, but he went ahead with his reckless decision.

Custer divided his men into three small groups. Captain Frederick Benteen would lead one group. Major Marcus Reno would lead another. According to Custer's plan, these two groups would prevent Sitting Bull from escaping. Custer himself would lead the third group, made up of about 200 men, in the central charge. This terrible mistake would doom them all.

Major Marcus Reno

A map showing the location of the Battle of the Little Bighorn

34

LAST STAND

The soldiers followed Custer's orders. Reno's group was quickly overwhelmed by hundreds of warriors. Benteen's group joined Reno's, and luckily, some of the men were able to retreat.

Chief Two Moons

Custer's group was left to face the furious Indians alone.

Sitting Bull was a medicine man, so he did not fight. Instead, Crazy Horse was aided by two other leaders, Chief Gall and Chief Two Moons. Custer's group moved in to attack. Soon, he realized that he and his men were outnumbered and in great danger. Custer tried to escape, but the mighty Sioux and Cheyenne

35

forced the soldiers higher into the hills above the Little Bighorn River.

Custer and his men were surrounded. The situation was desperate. As the Indians closed in, Custer ordered his men to **dismount**, shoot their horses, and hide behind the animal **carcasses** for protection. The idea didn't work.

Chief Gall, top. Custer being shot by the Sioux, bottom.

Only a scout named Curley (left) and a horse named Comanche survived the battle.

The Native American assault was vicious and quick. In less than an hour, every white man was dead or bleeding to death. Custer was last seen crawling for cover, bleeding from the mouth. He was later found with a bullet wound in his left temple. Some think Custer killed himself before the Indians could kill him.

Sitting Bull's vision of soldiers falling before the Sioux had come true. All that survived of the U.S. Army was one person and one animal—a scout named Curley and a horse named Comanche.

LAST VICTORY

Eleven days later, on July 6, the first report of the Battle of the Little Bighorn appeared in the *Bozeman Times*, a newspaper in Bozeman, Montana. Only days before, Americans had been celebrating the country's 100th birthday. This tragic news greatly changed their mood.

Most people were outraged. It was nothing new for Indians to be portrayed as bloodthirsty savages in the press—but this attack seemed especially brutal. People demanded that the government punish the Indians for their actions. Some of the Sioux, including Sitting Bull, fled to Canada. The army hunted down many of the others.

Most people believed that the Indians were the attackers at the Little Bighorn. They did not understand that the Native Americans simply wanted to live in peace and were protecting their homelands. In fact, the Indians were usually willing to share their land with newcomers. The Indians at Little Bighorn were defending themselves

38

The Sioux left the Battle of the Little Bighorn victorious.

against the unfair treatment they had suffered for centuries. The Battle of the Little Bighorn was one of the Native Americans' few victories in their long struggle with white settlers—but it was their last one. Little Bighorn is remembered as Custer's Last Stand, but it was the Indians' last stand too.

In 1877, the Sioux wars ended. Despite their bravery, the Indians had lost their lands. They were forced to leave their prairies and open spaces and squeezed onto small reservations, where the land was often poor and living conditions were miserable. Crazy Horse surrendered in September 1877. While in custody at a police station in Nebraska, he was stabbed in the back with a **bayonet** and died. In 1881, the government told Sitting Bull that he would be safe, so the chief returned to America. In 1885 he

Chief Crazy Horse's body is carried to its burial.

Chief Sitting Bull was killed on December 15, 1890.

joined Buffalo Bill's Wild West Show. Eventually the army ordered his arrest. He was shot to death by an Indian guard during a riot outside his cabin on a South Dakota reservation in 1890.

Lieutenant Colonel George Custer was given a military funeral at West Point on October 10, 1877. The horse Comanche—one of the two survivors—marched in parades of the Seventh Cavalry for years after the Battle of the Little Bighorn. In memory of the many who lost their lives on that famous battlefield, the horse carried a saddle, but no rider.

GLOSSARY

bayonet—a blade attached to the end of a rifle and used as a weapon in close combat

carcasses—the dead bodies of animals

cavalry—soldiers who ride horses

centennial—a 100th–anniversary celebration

court-martialed—put on trial for breaking military law

detachments—groups of soldiers chosen from a larger group

dismount—to get down from a horse

pronged—branched or forked

scout—a soldier who travels ahead of a military group to gather information about the enemy

skirmishes—small battles

testified—gave information under oath during a trial

treaty—a formal agreement between groups or nations

DID YOU KNOW?

- George Custer's autobiography *My Life on the Plains* was published in 1874, when Custer was only thirty-four years old.

- More than 200 men followed Custer into the Battle of the Little Bighorn but only one scout survived.

- The Battle of the Little Bighorn lasted about one hour.

- The Native Americans called George Custer "Yellowhair" or "Long Hair."

- The Sioux chief Crazy Horse got his name because a wild horse ran through his tribe's camp when he was born.

- At birth, Chief Sitting Bull was named Jumping Badger. His name was later changed to "Slow" or "Thoughtful One." He showed such courage in battle at age fourteen that his proud father renamed him again—giving him his own name, Sitting Bull.

- The Bureau of Indian Affairs, one of the oldest federal agencies in the United States, still exists.

IMPORTANT DATES

Timeline

1874	George Armstrong Custer violates a treaty with the Indians and enters the Black Hills in search of gold.
1876	The United States celebrates the centennial of the signing of the Declaration of Independence; Battle of the Little Bighorn takes place on June 25.
1877	Chief Crazy Horse surrenders and is killed in Nebraska; Custer's body is moved from its grave at the battle site and buried at West Point on October 10.
1879	Site of the Little Bighorn Battle becomes a national cemetery.
1890	Chief Sitting Bull shot to death.
1946	The battle site is named the Custer Battlefield National Monument.
1991	The battle site is renamed the Little Bighorn Battlefield National Monument and the U.S. government orders the building of an Indian memorial there.

IMPORTANT PEOPLE

GEORGE ARMSTRONG CUSTER

(1839–1876), *lieutenant colonel in the U.S. Cavalry*

CRAZY HORSE

(1842?–1877), *chief of the Oglala Sioux of the Black Hills*

GEORGE CROOK

(1829–1890), *officer in the Civil War and general who led the southern detachment of the three-pronged attack against the Sioux in 1876*

JOHN GIBBON

(1827? –1896), *colonel who led the eastern detachment of the three-pronged attack against the Sioux in 1876*

SITTING BULL

(1831? –1890), *chief of the Hunkpapa Sioux*

ALFRED H. TERRY

(1827–1890), *brigadier general who led the western detachment of the three-pronged attack against the Sioux in 1876*

WANT TO KNOW MORE?

At the Library

Ferrell, Nancy Warren. *The Battle of the Little Bighorn in American History.* Berkeley Heights, N.J.: Enslow, 1996.

Iannone, Catherine. *Sitting Bull: Lakota Leader.* Danbury, Conn.: Franklin Watts, 1999.

Krehbiel, Randy. *Little Bighorn.* Brookfield, Conn.: Twenty-First Century Books, 1997.

Schleichert, Elizabeth. *Sitting Bull: Sioux Leader.* Berkeley Heights, N.J.: Enslow, 1997.

Stein, R. Conrad. *The Battle of the Little Bighorn.* Danbury, Conn.: Children's Press, 1997.

Viola, Herman J. *It Is a Good Day to Die: Indian Eyewitnesses Tell the Story of the Battle of the Little Bighorn.* New York: Crown, 1998.

On the Web

Little Bighorn Associates

http://lbha.org/

For many links to sources of information about George Armstrong Custer, the Plains Indians, and the Indian Wars, including a link to the web site of the U.S. Seventh Cavalry

The Great Sioux Nation Picture Gallery

http://www.eagleswatch.com/great_sioux_nation.htm

Click on Great Sioux Nation Picture Gallery to see pictures of many chiefs of the Sioux Tribe

Midwest Archeological Center

http://www.mwac.nps.gov/

For photographs and information about the bullets, saddles, weapons, and other artifacts found buried at the site of the Battle of the Little Bighorn

Through the Mail

U.S. Army Military History Institute

22 Ashburn Drive, Carlisle Barracks

Carlisle, PA 17013-5008

For historical source materials, including articles and letters, relating to George Armstrong Custer, the Battle of the Little Bighorn, and other important people and events in U.S. Army history

On the Road

Little Bighorn Battlefield National Monument

P.O. Box 39

Crow Agency, MT 59022-0039

406/638-2621

INDEX

American Civil War, 14, *15,* 16
Arapaho Indians, 24, 31

Battle of Little Big Horn, 8, *9,* 39
Belknap, William, 26, *26*
Bell, Alexander Graham, 4, *5*
Benteen, Frederick, *32,* 33, 35
Black Hills, *10, 20,* 20–21, *30*
Bloody Knife (Native American scout), *30,* 31–32
Bozeman Times (newspaper), 38
Buffalo Bill's Wild West Show, 41
Bureau of Indian Affairs (BIA), 11

Cheyenne Indians, 24, 31, 35–36
Comanche (horse), 37, *37,* 41
Crazy Horse, chief of Oglala Indians, 24, 29, 35, 40, *40*
Crook, George, 25, *25,* 27, *27,* 29
Curley (Native American scout), 37, *37*
Custer, Elizabeth (wife), 17, *17*
Custer, George Armstrong, 7, *7,* 10, 14–16, *17,* 22, 26, 29, *30,* 31–33, 35–36, *36, 37,* 41

Dakota Indians. *See* Sioux Indians.

European exploration, 6

First Battle of Bull Run, 15, *15*

Gall (Native American chief), 35, 36
Gibbon, John, 25, 27, 29, 32
gold mining, *21,* 22
Grant, Ulysses S., 4, *4*

Hunkpapa Indians, 20, 24, *24*

Indian Removal Act, 10–11, 13
Indian Territory, 11, 13, 26

Lakota Indians. *See* Sioux Indians.
Little Bighorn River, 7, 24, 29, 36

map, *34*
Montana Territory, 8, 25

Native Americans, 5, 6, *6,* 8, *9,* 10–11, *12,* 13, 18–19, *18, 19,* 23–24, *28, 35, 36,* 38–40, *39, 40*

Oglala Indians, 20–21, 24

Reno, Marcus, 33, *33,* 35
reservations, 11, 22, 40
Rosebud Creek, 29

settlers, 8, 13, 18, 39
Sioux Indians, 19–20, *19,* 22, *23, 28,* 35–38, *36*
Sioux wars, 23, 40
Sitting Bull, chief of Hunkpapa Indians, 24, 25, *24,* 33, 35, 37, 38, 40, *41*
Sun Dance ceremony, *24,* 25

Terry, Alfred H., 25–27, 29, *31,* 32
Two Moons (Native American chief), 35, *35*

U.S. Army, 8, 20–21, 23, *23,* 25, 37
U.S. Cavalry, *12,* 13, 14

West Point military academy, 14, *14*

About the Author

Marc Tyler Nobleman has written seven books for young readers. He has also written for *The Great American History Quiz,* a History Channel program, and for several children's magazines, including *Highlights for Children.* Additionally, he is a cartoonist, and his single panels have appeared in more than forty magazines.